The Southern
Reaches

Also by Sherod Santos
Accidental Weather

The Southern Reaches

Sherod Santos

 Wesleyan University Press
Middletown, Connecticut

Grateful acknowledgment is made to the following periodicals in which poems
in this collection originally appeared (some in slightly different versions): *An-
taeus, The Antioch Review, The Atlantic Monthly, The Memphis State Review, The
Nation, The New Republic, New England Review/Bread Loaf Quarterly, The Paris
Review, Poetry, Poetry Canada Review, Quarterly West, The Yale Review.* "After
the Island Fighting," "At the All Clear," "Death," "The Enormous Aquar-
ium," "Homage to the Impressionist Painters," "Midsummer," and "Near the
Desert Test Sites" originally appeared in *The New Yorker.*

The Baudelaire epigraph is from a version of "Le Cygne," from *Imitations,*
by Robert Lowell, copyright © 1958, 1959, 1960, 1961 by Robert Lowell and
is reprinted by permission of Farrar, Straus & Giroux, Inc. and of Faber and
Faber Limited Publishers.

I would also like to thank the John Simon Guggenheim Memorial Foundation,
the Ingram Merrill Foundation, the Frost Place in Franconia, New Hampshire,
and the University of Missouri for their generous support while a large portion
of this book was written.

All inquiries and permissions requests should be addressed to the Publisher,
Wesleyan University Press, 110 Mt. Vernon Street, Middletown, Connecticut
06457

Library of Congress Cataloging-in-Publication Data
Santos, Sherod, 1948–
   The southern reaches/Sherod Santos.—1st ed.
     p.   cm.—(Wesleyan poetry)
   Bibliography: p.
   ISBN 0-8195-2159-0   ISBN 0-8195-1160-9 (pbk.)
   I. Title.   II. Series.
PS3569.A57S58   1989
811 .54—dc19   88-10231
                          CIP

Manufactured in the United States of America

This book is supported by a grant from the National Endowment for the Arts.

First Edition
Wesleyan Poetry

For my mother and father,
and for Benjamin Hart Santos

Contents

4. The Easter Manifestations

Its heart was full of its blue lakes, and screamed:
"Water, when will you fall?"
     —BAUDELAIRE, *The Swan*

1. An Illustrated Childhood

In the Rainy Season

The first signs of cloudbreak
In the mornings over Kolonia Cove
And we'd be up at the windows
Waiting while the mildewed air
Distilled through the wind-screens,
While the swollen, dun-colored
Canefields beyond, all runneled
With mud gullies and shallow
Green pools, brightened like bomb-
Burst in the sunshine: *Sun*-days!
And rainrust spilled from gashes
In the rocks of our garden wall,
And under the wet leaves splayed
In mud, the quaking, down-ticking
Blue thistle spurs lay like
Landmines along the footpath.
My brother and I would steal
Out then to a promontory hacked
Above a channel of the river
That emptied on the cove
And watch as the fishing boats
Came idling: dismasted and gal-
Vanized by the coruscating
Calms, their engines cannonaded
The shoreline where, heroically
Wounded, we'd level our broomsticks
On their bulwarks. Sea birds
Strafed the dragnets hung up drying
By the pier, and here and there
A column of smoke, a rampike
Harrowing the jungle. But it was
Only a matter of time before
We could hear it in the distance,
Like rice grains in a pan,

Or like a fusillade from a cross-
Fire of snipers, something
We could die of, if we'd had
Our way, braced and campaigning
From the blasted shore of that
Weak, white empire of childhood.

A Sunday Visit to Koalinga's

Being, I suppose, too young
For such things, I waited
Outside with a piebald cat
That kept scratching itself

Behind the ear—*that,*
As I remember, was the only
Sound I could hear except
For a horse cropping grass

Beneath a mangrove tree.
In the house itself (one
Of those abandoned estates
From the colonial days)

There was a curved flight
Of shallow steps that
Wound down from a glacis
To some ornamental stones

Where leaning at the hand-
Rail stood a barefooted
Girl whose hair was oiled
And braided straight back

Into many small ropelike
Plaits. She stood so
Still she might have been
Asleep and just dreaming

Us there, except that now
And then her hand went up
As if to wave hello, or
Write her name on the air:

Between us throbbed
The entire, blue, in-
Visible wilderness
Of that dead island hour.

When my brother, in time,
Stepped casually out
From the shade of an alcove
In the building next door,

I hid for a moment, and
Stared; and though he never
Turned around to look
At that girl, as we later

Climbed up to the spring-
Fed falls which thinned
Off into silence
In midair, I could smell

On his clothes
The lavish scent
Of pomade and lemon-
Blossom talc. And yet,

For all of that, he carried
A kind of lightness out
Onto the green and
Slippery steppingstones

(As though the body, I
Imagined, were *inside*
The soul): counter-
Balanced like a skater,

He leaned out over
The weir and dropped
A rock into the nothing-
Ness that was there.

And in the pool below,
A pool that seemed
Another world away,
The ripples turned over

Their careful copperplate,
And the noise
Of the parakeets ig-
Nited in the flame trees.

The Children of Paradise

At summer's end, a girl and I once
made it up unknowingly, the ritual,
    and the place forbidden
  beyond the boundary stones.
First we wrung a drop of blood
      from our pin-pricked thumbs,
    then swore an oath
through the wound: the bamboo

    scarecrow staked to a scarp
beside the pineapple fields
    would marry us in the eyes
of his indelible law, "Who go
here punished them good for
      to be sure." At midnight,
    under a staring moon,
we sprinted across the back

    half-acre the spinster-farmer
owned and hid ourselves
    among the family graves
  sheltered beneath a palm.
The headstones cooled our
      heaving backs, and breathed,
    it seemed, their mute, un-
dying alphabet of names;

    and through the palm's long-spiked
and feathery fronds, the planets
    hung like ancient bells
  whose sound had stirred the air
to lay its audible shadows
      around us. We were more alone
    than either of us
had ever been; and rubbed by

a brightness we could not see,
we began to feel
        we had entered the place
    of all secret and all
singing things: it was as though
            we'd stepped beyond
        the threshold of the world
to hold each other now

    differently, now closer together,
not weighing on ourselves, or in
        our arms. But we were
    children then, and so turning
our faces away from each other
            we began to feel, as children will,
        that inner, rank
seeping, like a blood trace

    on the tongue, which calls them up
from everywhere, and from
        all around us, rising
    like field music
from out of the ground, those darkly
            twinned spirits come
        lolling on the air
of our most intimate mistakes.

At the All Clear

That early in the morning
The village huts were still
Shuttered with silver,
Although, in the headlights,

A young woman appeared
Through an unhinged door
To be rubbing the night's
Sleep from her eyes.

The Red Cross truck was
Parked and driverless
Beside the Protestant
Church; and all along

The beaches the heaped
Debris of plantain
And carapace, seaweed,
And stripped palm fronds

Lay interlapped like
Parquet on the sand.
As our family and
Neighbors came down

From the high ground,
The souring heat un-
Focused the flyspecks
Floating in on the tide;

And the gulls which only
The day before had been
Blown back off
The breakers now scavenged

Along the shore, above
The dead-water outline
Of the pier. For days
To come there'd be

A shadow out over the coral
Shoals, an afterimage,
A shard of
Bottle glass pressed flat

In the palm. Our bungalow
Seemed to have been
Pulleyed up from a gash
In the ground: earth-

Spattered, prehistoric,
It stood there staggered
On its shaken stilts.
And yet how surprised

We were, each momentarily
Caught as if wondering
What to say at having
Found, inside, that nothing

Had changed, that the table
Was still set for an
Afternoon meal, and there
On the stove was a pot

Of red beans, and another
Of salted rice water.
It could've been
One of those places

We'd run across sometimes
In children's stories,
Where the world's familiar,
While remaining the same,

Will suddenly become
What it has never been,
A place you walk through
As if in dream:

The air barely rippled
Through the kitchen curtains
While Mother stood
Washing the unused plates,

While the winged ants beat
Against the light and
Dropped their transparent
Wings on the water.

After the Island Fighting
—*for my sister Cheri*

Our grandfather's hat stand's
Iron dowel drew off the heat
Through the louvered shades
When we came back in the evenings.

Outside, the agitated sea birds
Startled the air with their metal
Cries, the axe blows muted
By another inevitable "half-mile

Of clear," though now and then
We could hear a phrase
Exchanged between the men
Who were working there. Remember?

At six o'clock on the free market
Pier, when the dairy pails
Were filled and then hurried
Onto carts, how a mess of flies

Would throng around the ruff
That spilled their sides;
And how, if the rains
Didn't start before the beach

Was cleared, the heat burned in
Those milk-stain rings
With their vague insinuations
Of astronomy and power.

All but the brightest stones
Would darken in that hour,
First flickering a little before
Going out, like the village

Lanterns whose wicks weren't
Trimmed; and then, for the rest
Of the night, if the clouds
Blew in, or the moon

Wasn't out, the only color
We could see from our room
Was the phosphorous beam
From the government tower

Lying on the water like a piece
Of thread, we decided once,
Which the sun itself had wet and
Slipped through a needle's eye.

Waiting to Be Restationed

Small bundles of rotting vines smoked beside
The beanfields, bells had called the sardine boats
Back into shore, and the braziers were lit
That had nearly blackened the tufa walls.

Fish scales glittered on the abandoned stalls,
And everywhere then the smell of limestone
Blended with peppers and olive oil, smoke
And dung; and how often we'd stand there, bored

With everything by late afternoon, stand
At the hotel window watching, as though
From an empty waiting room, while the sun
Wandered off through the hills. And some evenings

We'd stand so long staring out into those
Gradually emptying streets, it seemed
The streets themselves were something we desired:
The thin shadows below the olive groves

Drifting downhill toward the abandoned square,
The leaves combing slowly the mild sea air.

The Air Base at
Châteauroux, France

In the American schoolyard
where we lunged headfirst
onto the rocky ground scrab-
bling for a ball
                    as if
for love, the crossed chalk–
line still electrified our
tough boyish hearts, and no
one much cared
                    for such
exotic gods as loomed up
out of the Palatine Hills
in the required guidebooks
dumped in heaps
                    behind our
makeshift goal. We knew
what we knew. Sweatstains
darkened our blue school
shirts while
                    our fathers'
fighters strafed the mock-
ups in the practice fields,
never far enough from town
it didn't thunder
                    all day
through the blackened
cottages' stony stares locked
up tight behind their shot
bolts; nor through

                    the evening,
either, when drifting home,
stripped to the waist, we'd
dance feet-chalked across
the marketplace
                    like young,
uneasy gods, a little drunk
on our shame, our power.

The Gypsy Carnival

The long wooden benches were packed with men from
   The surrounding towns, working men mostly,
     Farmhands and mechanics, and here
    And there some father who'd decided it was
  Time to take his son to see the sun-struck fantasy
    Of a name tacked up on kiosks

In all the squares, "La Fleur, Madame Orchidée."
   But stepping into the tent in street
     Clothes, and dropping a needle
    Onto a record, she turned to that room of
     Rough whispering men and smiled
In a kind of welcome: her smile like a skipped stone

Skimmed that lake of faces, her lips parted, and while
   Her tongue traced out the line of her mouth,
     The thin-kohled eyes drew every-
    One into focus, one at a time, and held
Them there in a lowering light until the expression
    On each face dropped away, as if

Suddenly overcome by fatigue. From then on only she
   Touched everything she did, but swayed by
     Another music none of us could hear,
    A music opening through the body of someone
     At home undressing in the kitchen
After work: unbuttoning her blouse with a sigh, then

Slipping the skirt, and down around the garters, her
   Clothes a soft rubble gathering at her feet
     The faint, unpetaled stink of her.
    Then, at last, naked, bored and empty-handed,
She rose back more eagerly along her buttocks, breasts
    And arms, fingering and pinching,

Embracing herself, wanting to be warmed, and now
     Turning to the room that could warm her;
         But no one moved, and no one ever
     Really thought he would until she shivered up
         Before one old man no taller than
A boy and bent back slowly away from him, his hand

Unfolding out to her like a pathetic pink flower just
     Opening on the sun; and a feeling in her must've
         Passed through him when she tossed
     Her hair and bent back farther, like a lithe
Tree thumbed over by the wind, gathering the air, until
     Everyone there could feel it too,

That following rush just lengthening out inside of her,
     And now nothing could stop her as she arched
         Back deeper onto her outspread
     Hands, dragging the sawdust with her hair,
         Then grabbing her ankles, taking
Hold of herself and pulling back through, like a wave

Plunged into its chamber, like a body enfolded
     By the soul, until finally, inevitably,
         Her face appeared, puffed and up-
     Ended through a shock of curls, and smiled,
Who knows, to forgive us all, men and boys, fathers
     And sons, all silently looking

Away from her when that still uncertain music stopped,
     The needle ground off its groove, and everyone
         Stood up stumbling for the aisle,
     The flush of blood a sudden sun-dazed impulse
         In the brain, and the 90 degrees
Inside shredding the dull light around the tent flaps.

Farmland Beside the Loire

The cold spring
rains had come
early to the bean-
fields, the pools
of standing water
slowly leveling
the rows, the wind
green-scented with
the wild grass
blowing there be-
side the running
ditch. After three
weeks the mist had
gone, the last thin
wisps drawn off
like topsails out
of the tree limbs:
now the grackles
were nesting there,
their plicate tails
working at the air
sliding like deep
water toward
evening, and now
the windows of
the drying sheds
stayed lit all
night with acety-
lene lamps, their
canted roofs
glowing beneath
the moon as though
a sea-salt inked
its phosphor in
for good, as

though, even there,
the huge, unbroken
whale bones rose,
silent and shadow-
less through the
rippling ground.

2. The Sea Change

Driving Out of the Keys

White heat, and heat waves riffling the asphalt's
Glare—the car's the pivot around which turn
These sprawling fields, retarded by summer
And bleached out featureless beneath a farflung
Sky. For the last two hours, my wife has leaned
Her head against the door, her hand held up
To shield her eyes, as though, as we drove
Straight through into the late afternoon,
The unblinking O of oblivion had lifted
From the road and fixed itself, irrevocably,
In that bright blindspot pulsing on the windshield.

What we imagine outside may not even exist:
A patch of cloud floating on the horizon
Might make and unmake a small island of its own;
And all around the landscape might become
Some world we walked away from years ago,
The things of that world called back again
Out of the rising rubble of the air—
The rusted husk of an automobile smoldering
Like a match-head snuffed out in a hand,
The tar-papered shanties shuttered with foil,
The oil drums and billboards and roadside stands—

And everything, for a moment, seems both familiar
And strange, and everything takes on
A meaning that involves our coming here, and our
Going away. And so it is that mile after mile
Some feeling begins to take hold in us, rising
Seamless through the warm floorboards, then settling
Behind the eyes which at this hour, as the sun
Burns down, are looking for something, though
We don't know why, in that pale flame color filling
The sky, or crossing a bridge, in that boy below,
Drifting in a pirogue on the livid stream.

Betrayal

There were two of you in the dream, you
And another woman, both intimate and apart
As in the circle of a lens, and both seated
In identical, high, cane-backed chairs
Out in a garden where the redbuds and asters
Formed a backdrop so still, my unexpected
Presence throbbed on the footpath like some
Gross and inexplicable flower. Then I came
Forward: I could almost feel the wheel
Of the seasons turn in your heart, almost feel
Your strained indifference through that thick,
Noon, summery air. Then a door shut quietly
Behind me; then the rain gauge made a click
Like a key in a lock. It seemed the idle
Atmosphere sweltered around the sundial and our
Ardor, so you, as if tired of waiting for the theme
To that hour, reached out toward the woman
And ran a hand through her hair. Then a palm
Tree in the garden began to sway its head,
And the voice which caressed her was my own.

Midsummer

Late in the day, the sun-
Enameled wavelets softening,
The heat dying slowly
Along the motel's beach-side

Redwood deck, and you step bare-
Armed and lipsticked out
Among the potted
Fuchsia's breakneck flowers

Sculling on the breeze,
And watch, a moment,
As the pelicans out beyond
The breakers tack up

Over the swells, then
Drop down pick-
Axe hard
Like a sudden outburst

In the quiet air. And I
Am reminded then of
Propertius'
Furious, flax-haired Cynthia

Driving down the Tiber
Behind her white,
Clipped cobs, the woman
In whom, as in some shadowy

Door, he'd found love's
Dark other left
Loitering, pungent-sweet,
Unbuttoned a little

And slick with desire,
With eyes like black florets
At the center
Of a ruff. We stood

Eye-level with the white-
Wash as it lunged
And reddened up
The pebbled sand, earth-

Drawn, pined-for, all strain
And freshening, and, not
About to set things right
Or wrong, we held

Our peace, and before too long
It was twilight still
Winnowing the shore
Of our sure, small heat.

Inspiration

Say what we will, at times it seems the rarest
Moments, the most splenetic trills, the most
Ecstatic gestures, are conceived in sloth
And degradation and executed by a great unstaggered
Surge of feeling which bursts forth suddenly
Like a yard given over to day lilies, surprise lilies,
Naked ladies, to the spiked, thumbed, overlooked
Phallus of the yucca plant, to the carmined
Secret of the flowering dogwood's uninfected petals
Falling around you sunbathing naked in the grass
Like Susanna among the Elders, to the goat-horned
Furl of the climbing fern, to the certain posture
The May apple chooses to display itself, to the heart-
Raking itch of wood lice in the oak, to the coming
Darkness, to the secret balance, to the extreme
And desolate flowering of the night-blooming cereus,
And to all those things, all that loosestrife,
Spiderwort, tickweed and flax, all those hidden
Gothic amplitudes which leave us finally,
Tattooed and senseless, trembling on the stair.

Married Love

As they sat and talked beneath the boundary trees
In the abandoned park, neither one mentioning
Her husband, or his wife, it seemed as though
Their summer shadows had detached themselves
In the confusion of those thousand leaves: but no more
Than they could call those shadows back from the air,
Could they ignore the lives they had undone,
And would undo once more that afternoon
Before giving in to what they knew, had always known.
And yet, in turning away, what they would say was not
That thing, but something else, that mild excuse
That lovers use of how things might have been
Had they met somewhere else, or in some better time,
Were they less like themselves than what they are.

Midwest Dusk

From far away a dog's
bark carries across
this year's cash crop,
soybeans, a ribbed
grisaille in the spur
of light left candling
the rock quarry's lime-
stone trench. Bull-
horned, treehorned,
the horizon closes on
the farmsteads huddled
in their warm, well-
lighted, companion-
able air, and now
the world is locked
and still, a beanleaf
recoiled into its
split-stitched seed;
but think, instead,
through an uncurtained
window of an ordinary
night in the middle
of July: a refrigerator
humming, an upstairs
desklamp softening
this month's unpaid
bills, and at the just-
cleared kitchen table,
cards turned over so
quietly in a game
of Patience beginning
again, that bright
over the dark verge
the Dog Star rises
without the moon.

Work

Pushing off on her back out
Into the fishpond's cold
Archaic glitter, my naked wife
Could not have guessed how

High she rode into the noon
Sky, a brightened polestar
Gliding out between nothing
And nothing, between a sun-

Lit vacancy and its ancient,
Reflected, weightless
Hour unrippling back
From the sedges. The just-

Cut grasses fumed around her
Like gasoline, a few
Spent bees dozed above
The compost, and in my arms

The steady *thrum* of the mower
Carried on, though I'd
Shut it off to sit down
And watch: but so fond of her,

The water parted to take
Her back from that aimless
Sky, where light-
Headed and slippery as a star

She turtled under the still
Simmering Indian summer
To startle the sunfish
At the margins—then punctured

Back with a blow-frog's gasp,
An amazed stranger
Conjured into the world
By a willow shadow

Spread out on the grass
Like an extravagant Old
World gesture no
One believes in anymore.

On that stalled shore she climbed
Back out among the cool
And slightly washed-
Out leaves to towel off,

Put on her clothes, and shake
Her hair out in no time
Which slips off into the past,
Or future, into nothing

But the pure unburnished hum-
Drum of that moment, that place,
From which we turned away
Eventually and went back to work.

3. The Art of Fiction

The Enormous Aquarium
(after Proust)

All morning long from inside the lobby
Of the Grand Hotel, the empty seashore
Hung suspended there like a tapestry
Of no particular interest or value,
And it was only at intervals, while cards
Were shuffled and dealt around the fours,
That one of the players, finding nothing
To do, might turn his head to glance outside
At an occasional sail on the horizon.
And so, too, the afternoon hours, immutable
And bland, would pass before the windows
That more and more, as the sun declined,
Came to seem like mirrors in which you look
And find no other face but your own.

But then the evening arrived, the heat
Of the day settled onto the sand,
And suddenly it happened—as though
At the gesture of an imaginary hand—
That a great hidden stream of electricity
Would flood the dining rooms and halls
Until the hotel became, in its alluvial glow,
Like an enormous aquarium against whose
Glass the fishermen's and the tradesmen's
Families, clustering invisibly in the outer
Dark, would press their faces to look in.
And how like strange fishes the occupants
Now seemed as they floated past on those
Golden eddies of unrippling light: there,

A Serbian officer whose organdy plume
Was like the blow of spume off some great
Blue whale; and there, a young man who,
From his earliest years, had obviously moved
In the freshest waters of Faubourg Saint-Germain;
Or there, grand and aloof, the dowager Duchess,
Her powdered jaws closing on a morsel
Of food like a primitive shellfish closing
On a spore. . . . And the question now lingering
In the air was how the glass could sustain
A world so vastly different from the poor,
A world where tea gowns and sable, grosgrain
And crepe de Chine, topaz and silver
And the enameled ring that encircled a wrist

All spoke of a life grown infinitely
Distant and unreal. Yet if, from out
Beneath the eaves, the unwearying, gentle
Flight of the sea-martins and swallows
Had not arisen just then—one beyond another,
To shiver the air like a playing fountain,
Like dying fireworks strewn out along
The shore—without the sudden lull
Of that brief interruption, they might easily
Have stayed much later at the glass,
Instead of turning, as they did, beneath
A disc of moon as round and white as an eye,
To walk back home down the darkened streets
Like some ancient and magnificent tribe.

Homage to the Impressionist Painters

Two small boys crouched beside
A remote-control panel
In the Luxembourg
Gardens are guiding their

Nuclear submarine down
Beneath the crowded waters
Of the sailing-pond; because
It's Sunday, and early

In May, there are countless
Children, and the gardens
Are filled with a laughter
And shouting that could al-

Most sound, if you closed
Your eyes, like the furious
Confusions of a battle.
But the bordering roses are

Sorbet pinks, and the leaves
Of the chestnuts so pale-
Ly green they seem formed
From seawater and plankton;

So that down the long
Tunnels of the promenades,
The slow rental ponies
Are painted with a shade

That increases their shyness
And importance. A uni-
Cyclist turning figure eights
In the sand, and the usual

Circle of men playing *boules,*
And a group of white-
Frocked teenage girls—young
Apprentice surgeons? or

Meat-market clerks?—
With flecks of blood high up
On their sleeves. And
Out in a glade cordoned off

With chains (like Paradise,
It's not to walk on but there
To see) a woman has spread a blue
Bed sheet and placed a rock

At each corner—she smiles
At the world from her place
In the world, and she is not
Changed, nor should she be,

By the sudden, ecstatic cry
That says: Open your eyes,
The sky's overhead, the treetops
Are swimming through the warm

Spring air, and the instant
Of death is just rising
In the pond, where all is lovely,
And crazy, and contrived.

Death
(after Elizabeth Bowen)

Although great in passing, although suddenly enlarged
    The frightened heart puts up its proud defense,
        Still, it always leaves you feeling
    A little smaller somehow, and living becomes a little
        Meaner then, necessitous, and preoccupied
With harder pleasures, like the lives of the poor.

It's as though your childhood house had been gutted
    By fire, the blackened walls left standing,
        The windows gaping under an open sky,
    And suddenly one day you find yourself standing out
        On the lawn without the heart or ambition
To rebuild. And in that hour, with its one idea

Of releasing you from some part of yourself, you think
    You can see it unfolding there: how the maple trees
        That line the yard are all cut down,
    The land itself sold out in parts, how before
        Too long small apartments will appear
In a long red row, each one a home for someone

You don't know. And after dark, where once was silence,
    The maples' shadows drawn slowly across
        The grass by a moon in counterpoise
    Against the night, you find, instead, a string
        Of porchlights have come on like stars,
And the bluish glow of television screens has filled

The windows from street to street. And then it happens
    That in your mind a gate will click, a door swing
        Shut, and bicycling children drift home
    Like birds from the avenues and the birdless dark,
        Until your childhood house seems gone
For good into the dead center of some memory's glow.

But years from now, when the smell of spring is still
   Sweet in the air, or when snowdrops are beginning
     To gather under the palings, when the blue
   Autumn first blurs the narrow streets, or the low
     Sun in winter dazzles the windows gold,
You'll discover inside, in that vague way you're still

Drawn to the air, that something has remained, something
   Which, now silent and unseen, still touches
     The heart. And there is someone, too,
   Someone perhaps just returning from work, who will
     Pause a moment, in sorrow or love, a hand
On the apartment gate, but not to wonder: What was here?

The Unsleeping Genius of Misfortune

If ever there was a story
whose subject was Paradise
        and whose theme was its loss,
    it was his: it was 4 A.M.,
a screen door was banging
        in an abandoned house at the end
    of the street, and time
after time the neighbor's

    watchdog hurled itself against
its metal chain; and even as
        it was so late in the year,
    the old blown leaves kept
scuffing the pavement with
        their paper shoes, annoyed,
    it seemed, to have come
this far just to find themselves

    in some sleepless hour, adrift
in an air still summery
        with the thought of her.
    And who would not think,
just to know how it feels,
        that the man who was lying
    in bed awake and the woman
whose absence stood round him

    in a ring were both tonight so
nearly composed of the world
        outside that to be there
    was enough to awaken, like
a sound, that time which
        time brings back to them.
    And yet, how little
that all really mattered

to the man, or the fact that
his story might become
        one day an occasion for
    the woman to disappear
into a presence she'd
        discover was all her own,
    as if the lover within her
were Eve herself, and Adam

    the lover within him. But isn't
that, after all, our old
        habit of dreaming? To find
    late at night that someone
has come to lie down in
        our beds, someone who, unable
    to sleep, begins telling
the story of two people

    whose lives have grown apart
from each other,
        and telling it in a way
    that sounds familiar
at first, until gradually
        we see it's really us
    that person is talking about,
though what we remember

    we could not have seen:
how the banging door
        has changed itself into
    an axehandle hammered
on a board, how the watchdog's
        become a broken cup
    out on the lawn, how the leaves
have turned, as if it's true,

into a playground of children
holding hands in a ring.
     And so it was, giving up
   to the story, that the man
awake finally closed
         his eyes and lay perfectly
     still, until his mind made
sunrise, and he slept.

The Art of Fiction
(after Hardy)

It's the way each evening unfolds the same,
The way the old men in shirtsleeves come out
To play *boules* beneath the chestnut trees,
The way the shopkeepers linger in their doorways
To talk, while out on the steps the women
With their children fan themselves gazing off
Toward the square, where arm in arm
The lovers stroll past, indifferent, it seems,
They are so alone. And it's the way it all
Happens so effortlessly—a little twilight
Is all it takes, and the bored village boys
Stop spinning their bicycles in the sandlot
Dirt and start hanging around the fountain
And watching. But on this particular evening,
The woman they are watching they don't
Understand: pacing the sidewalk near the bus
Station doors, she smokes and stares and
Pushes back her hair in a gesture they find
So unlike desire, they can't imagine
Undressing her there, for all their remarks
And sharp glances. But suppose the world,
As it will at times, decided tonight
To explain such things. Suppose the woman
Eventually stepped out
                           from the curb
And stopped a man passing by in the street;
And suppose the man at first drew back
From her, so that the silence around them
Grew suddenly so large that everyone
Nearby was drawn nearer. Then suppose,
In that moment, we could hear her say,
"I've been looking for you. I thought
We could try to make it up somehow. I
Miss you at home. Come back there."

Then the silence again. Then the answer:
"No," he says, "it's too late now. And besides,
You know, there's another woman and all.
You should've thought about that a lot sooner."
A pause: then there seemed no more to say.
Then suppose the man walked off toward
The square and left the woman still standing
In the street. And suppose the woman just
Stood there, without moving, for so long
That everyone around her turned back to find
The evening had passed, the sky had gone black,
And one by one bright stars had come out
That care nothing, of course, for the sorrow
Of men's wives, or anyone else, for that matter.

4. *The Easter Manifestations*

Empire
(Luxembourg Gardens, 1986)

And yet how quietly it all begins
Filling with wet light the circling paths
Fronted by plane trees and pedestaled air:
This Saturday, like a sunken ship hauled
To the surface, its damaged hull traversed
By fish now drying splendored with coins
And ore. The children huddle around their
Rented boats, the adults at their novels,
And stone lions leap across the fountain-
Spray to shake the toque in the ungloved hand
Of a Medici who has lost her head
To the lily pads dragging the bottom.
And yet it all comes, the peals of laughter
From the pony carts, steam from the storm grates
Threading through the trees, the smell of *gaufres*
And diesel fumes, and the clouded windows
Of the palace struck blind against the sun,
It all comes and passes, pigeon-winged, up-
Gathered, ephemeral into the air,
Before the mind, before the slow-rolling
Constellations can watermark the glare.

Photograph of My Father
(Public Gardens, Berlin, 1948)

The sun's suspended like a drop of amber
Above the crescent of a colonnade,
And he is standing on a gravel path
Between turned-up rows of empty flower beds.

And all around the world's gone gray, like a lapse
In memory, or like a charcoal sketch
That was left behind in some unused drawer
So long ago that all of its small details—

The young mothers and prams and pigeons feeding
Beneath the linden trees—have finally
Smudged away. Except: how he's raised his hand
In just this way, as if from beyond the frame

Of that afternoon he would wave to a world
That was after he was. And in that wave
The soft corrugations of those massive
Clouds are moving again, and the upturned earth

Is trembling still from the troop trains passing
Just off to one side, trailing small bits of ash.

Nineteen Fifty-five

After all the late suppers of that faraway
Summer at his grandparents' house,
He would wait outside on the screened
Back porch with the screams of the blue jays
Plundering in the trees, and the sun-drunk
Yellowjackets droning, and he would count
The minutes backwards until the world
Grew distant, like the ocean inside
A shell. But that day dull, gray and
Heavy-headed clouds had risen unexpectedly

Into the evening sky, and he hadn't seen
The dark begin to spread across
The lawns and bushes, and he was afraid
At first and so went indoors
To sit in the kitchen while the coffee
Was poured, and the dishes were put back
In the cupboards. Then almost just as
Suddenly, he was quiet again, and happy,
And he wondered at the way the light
From the kitchen formed a glimmering square

That lay out on the side yard, a square
In which he could see played back, as on
A movie screen, small things he'd felt himself
Feel that day: the smoke from the coal
Train winding through the hills,
The cat's milk soured and yellowing
In its bowl, his new shoes crackling
Down the gravel drive while the eyes
Of a stranger who'd paused at the gate
Watched him without speaking in the morning.

It was the hour when a hush settles over
A town, when porches darken and voices
Bloom in drowsy clouds above the rooftops,
And much as he might have wanted to then,
He could not stop that flood
Of things, and he thought of the earth
As a sphere that spun in a crazy arc
That looped and hung, while the planets
Coursed, and the moon and sun
Moved through the star lanes unchanging.

For the earth was somehow different from them,
With all its facts and histories,
Its scalloped oceans and desert sands,
Its flowers and rains and long seasons
Of trouble, with its wars he'd heard called
Beautiful names—"Korean" and "Roses"
And "Holy." And he thought of the shuffle
Of soldiers' feet, thousands of soldiers
With dumbstruck eyes, and of the spiraling
Planes and overturned carts he'd seen

In magazines and movies; and he thought
Of the cities all over the globe, cities
Bombed into streets and burning, and as
He whispered their names he could feel
On his tongue the terrible impermanence
Of nations: *Bangkok* and *London, Guernica*
And *Rome, Dresden* and *Moscow* and *Hiroshima.*
But they were names he was still unable
To see except in small and momentary glimpses
Of things, of a woman kneeling in the rubble

Beside a horse whose belly had been ruptured,
Of a man hunched over a wood-spoked
Wheel in a frozen ditch in the tundra,
Of a naked girl whose head had been shaved
And who was tied to a chair in the middle
Of a crowd that milled about her like
Shoppers. . . . All this time the boy had sat
Tilting forward in his straight-backed chair,
His elbows on the table for balance,
And he felt in his throat there were unknown

Words that would never in his lifetime
Get spoken, never be given a name,
And he was afraid to think he might
Take them away, take them away forever
Into that black and dividing night even now
Unraveling the edges of the light
That fell in a golden square
From the window. So he turned his head
Away from the glass, and let his chair
Tip back to the floor, and just beyond

His outspread hands there were dark coffee
Circles that had deepened to stain, and flies
Had settled in quiet rings, which were all
I'd remember thirty years from then
When rising from dinner with my wife
And son, news of warships gathering
In the Gulf was broadcast on the radio
In the kitchen—and the kitchen,
Whose windows had blurred from within,
Would grow ludicrous before it grew dim.

Near the Desert Test Sites
(Palm Desert, California)
—for Logan and Renée Jenkins

Unlike almost everything
Else just surviving here
In summer, poison flowers
Flourish in this sweltering
Heat, tangling like blown
Litter in fences around
The trailer parks and motel
Pools, and turning the islands
Pinkish-white between
Divided lanes of freeway,
Where all day long against
The burnished hubbub of U-
Haul trucks and automobiles,
Off-the-road vehicles and
Campers, the oleander shakes
Its brightly polished pocket-
Knives, as at the motorcade
Of some ambassador hurrying
Through a village of the poor.
And every day by late after-
Noon the overwatered lawns
Around the shopping mall
Still burn off brown, their
Pampered opulence upbraided
By the palms' insomniac
Vision of one ineffable apoc-
Alyptic noon. But the smell
Is somehow sweeter than
That makes you think, a dry
Lemon-sweetness, as if some-
Where nearby wild verbena

Has been forced to leaf
By a match held up to each
Bud—and the silo-skyscraper
Holiday Inn at the famous
Resort "Where the Horizon
Ends" could almost be that
Match the way the heat
Sloughs off it like after-
Burn. And yet, because
Of the way the sun in-
Tensifies everything, one
Always has the feeling there
Is much less here than meets
The eye: the halcyon blink
Of a shard of glass, a Lear-
Jet wafted into vapor out
On the tarmac's run, the way
Common quartzstone gives
Off heat which seems to come
From inside itself, and not,
In fact, from that more-
Than-imaginably-nuclear sun
Which every morning starts
Up so illusionless, and every
Evening slow-dissolves
On the blue and otherwise
Planetary hills, like a Valium
Breaking up on the tongue.

The Neurophysiology
of Fear

In the human brain
there have been dis-
covered tiny spaces
between linked nerve
cells, gaps, which
the neurophysiologist
C. S. Sherrington in
1897 called synapses.
When a nerve impulse
reaches a gap—say, you
decide to take a walk
on the pier after work,
it's late in the evening,
and you hear below, as if
never before, the low
sucking of the surf
against the pilings—
what happens then
is that tiny packets of
a thousand or fewer neuro-
transmitter molecules
release, like a flood
of feeling, their con-
tents into the synapse:
the molecules then diffuse
across the connecting
cell and lock on tightly
to its surface receptors,
just as though each one
really wanted to be
by itself for a while. In
some cases, this simple
desire will open up
channels in the adjoining
cell to permit inside

electrically charged atoms
which, like thoughts
themselves, are forever
present in the space
around the nerve cells.
If enough packets
are finally released,
and enough channels
are opened—if, for
example, you were also
to see on your evening
walk the mica glitter
of the rising moon,
and out on the horizon
escort ships from the
Pacific Fleet drifting
like ice floes down the
Americas—the recipient
cell will in turn become
either stimulated or in-
hibited, the organism
funneled into history or
withdrawn altogether
from its perceptions of
what we call pleasure
and pain: it's as though
while standing at the end
of the pier, and with no
one but yourself beside
you there, you decided
to close your eyes and
let, not the moment out,
but that trawled, star-
littered sea-surge in.

Genetics

Earlier today, wandering around in the once-
Sweet upstairs dark of our next-door neighbors'
Abandoned house, I discovered back behind
A collapsed bedstead a pack rat nested in
A cardboard box which had ANNA's! KEEP OUT!
Crayoned along its sides, and a child's
Crude skull-and-crossbones beneath it.

Two pink, stoned eyes stared into the flashlight
And would not budge until I moved in closer
With a piece of lath to nudge it out
Of its squatter's camp: it never fails
To interest us, the evicted's world, even one
Made up, as this one was, of broomstraw,
Shoestring, a scrap of tin, what appeared to be

The chewed-up reed of a clarinet, a hairpin,
Pop-top, the four linked spheres of a brass
Lampchain, a dime, a glassbead, and all
Suspended in the weave of some far-fetched
Warp of lint and twine, and like a love letter
Shredded out of anger and tears, tiny wads of light
Pink paper shot electric through the clutter.

And yet at a certain distance it wasn't really
Clutter at all, but an aggregate of what's
Lost and found, a fibrous, fist-sized thicket
Like the human brain collaged with the salvage
Of forgetfulness and dream, and still composing
A past to present us with: some miniature empire
Of what we've been, uprooted like a tuber from memory.

It was as if from the shambles of the pack rat's
World a self was begun, some not-yet-
Realized prospect for a life, derivative
And varying, yet cohering in a kind of
Neurobiological network built so tenuously
Around one consciousness, one almost
Wonders we survive it there, in the pathos

Of those lost, discarded things, in that skein
Of intelligence, that sweet and sadly
Nourished illusion that, our own lives
Over, something else will take them up,
Something that maybe doesn't care for us
But that treasures nonetheless the mindless
Flotsam of what we were. And leaning closer

Still, and burrowing down deeper disturbing
That precarious interior's heart, I found,
Underneath, Scotch-Taped along its edges,
And fixed very carefully to the center
Of the box, the reason, perhaps, for Anna's
Stern injunction to the world: a folded,
Blue, watermarked sheet of loose-leaf paper

Which opening disclosed, in an ecstatic,
Looping, left-handed scrawl: "I, Anna
Rosalie Martin LOVE Cesar Romero Douglas
More than anything else in the world!"

Muséum National d'Histoire Naturelle, Paris

And yet nothing ever seems
quite so strange as our
    natural history, that laddered
series of dispossessions
    we now, looking down on, reclaim.

All the same it's still one
of those places we go to
    half expecting to find some
not quite happy secret
    about ourselves, some plain

unspoken parable of origins
which, if we ever made
    it out, would make us feel,
like a puzzle piece,
    a small part of the unknown.

It's there I took my son
today, into that immense,
    impersonal, and vaulted space
where the bones of millennia
    lattice up the mullioned windows

arched cathedral high. And though
we'd only gone to look
    at the room full of dinosaurs
and whales, we found
    ourselves coming back to see

the section on comparative anatomy.
My son is not yet two
    years old, and he only speaks
the simplest words, but "Look!"
    his eyes kept saying to me

dreaming before the glass,
"Look: *les monstres humains,*"
    just as though their pain
were finally much less real
than our wonder could ever be.

But there were more of them
than any boy his age
    could hold in his mind
at once, and he'd stood there
staring past the sill to a world

    disfigured beyond his dreams,
so quickly he drifted
    from case to case, drawing
his fingers behind him
on the glass, and only once

    did it seem, though I can't
be sure, that something
    inside of that sad display
held him long enough
that a stillness within them

touched a stillness in him.
For he paused a moment and
    drew closer to see a little
girl who was actually two,
    in fact, and both of them named,

    Hélène-Hortense and Marie-Lucille,
and both of them joined
    down the center of the skull,
just as though, at that
moment, they had leaned so close

so that they might keep their
secret from this boy
        whose blond-haired head inclined
    toward that necessary
        suffering our bodies form.

The Easter Manifestations

A woman who'd been watching
From a fifth-floor room kept
Mouthing, as I passed, what
Appeared to be an enormous

Yawn, or a warning, though
Her much-pierced window
Curtains bellied in the wind
So one couldn't really tell

The difference. And for
The rest of the day, a sense-
Less order filled the streets
Like the smell of gunpowder

With its reddish weight
In the air. In the entryway
To an English bookstore
Near the Arènes de Lutèce,

There was a wooden chair
On which a tripod telescope
Stood gazing through the air
With the utter detachment

Of a soul; and up in the trees
Of a pin-oak forest
In the Jardin des Plantes,
There were a dozen naked body

Casts (both men and women, all
Middle-aged) which had been
Injected, as the poster
Explained, with a chlorophyll

Solution that turned them all
Into living plants, like
Living people climbing there.
Except that's not the way that

People really climb in trees,
So hopefully, their heads up-
Lifted toward the highest
Limbs as though each had left

Some precious thing in those
Topmost leaves, a thing,
Or so they'd have us
Believe, so fragile and so

Clear to them (like a private
Image each carried inside
Of a Paradise where there are
No trees) they've had to take off

All their clothes to even
Try and reach it there. And
Yet, only twenty yards away,
A huge bronze bear's been trying

For half a century to squeeze
The life out of a trapper
Who's just killed
One of her cubs. And farther

Still, down along the Quai
De Bercy, a snub-nosed tug-
Boat struggled past dragging
An empty coal barge back,

Like the beautiful wreckage
Of a carnival float; or like
Unamuno's dual illusions,
Hope and Memory—the one

The shadow over what's to come,
The other over some still
Unimaginable past—which
Will not leave us reconciled.

Notes

1. An Illustrated Childhood

Because that's how they're remembered, the islands of the first section are no doubt something of a composite of Oahu (Hawaii), Pohnpei (Micronesia), and Guam (Oceania).

3. The Art of Fiction

The setting and central metaphor of "The Enormous Aquarium" are adapted from Proust's *Remembrance of Things Past,* particularly from the second book, *Within a Budding Grove,* and from my own recollections of a visit, as a child, to the Grand Hotel on Mackinac Island.

Similarly, "Death" is indebted to Elizabeth Bowen's *To the North,* though the house I had in mind was a family home (Greenville, South Carolina), which burned to the ground in 1961.

4. The Easter Manifestations

For the technical information about the human brain in "The Neurophysiology of Fear," I have relied on Israel Rosenfield's essay, "The New Brain."

The figures in the trees in "The Easter Manifestations" were part of an anonymous exhibit entitled "Les Arboriginées," which opened in Paris in the spring of 1984. That same year there were a number of demonstrations in and around the Latin Quarter, one of which (where police response had been especially violent) immediately preceded the time of the poem.

ABOUT THE AUTHOR

Sherod Santos has won a number of awards and fellowships, including, among others, the Delmore Schwartz Memorial award, a "Discovery"/ *The Nation* award, the Oscar Blumenthal prize from *Poetry* magazine, an Ingram Merrill grant, a Pushcart prize, a Guggenheim fellowship, and an NEA grant. He was named poet-in-residence at the Robert Frost Place in Franconia, New Hampshire, for 1984. His first book, *Accidental Weather*, published in 1982, was a National Poetry Series selection. He has published, in addition, two chapbooks.

Santos is a graduate of San Diego State University (B.A. 1971, M.A. 1974), the University of California at Irvine (M.F.A. 1978), and the University of Utah (Ph.D. 1982). He won three awards from the Utah Arts Council. He is associate professor of English at the University of Missouri-Columbia. Santos lives in Columbia, Missouri.

ABOUT THE BOOK

The Southern Reaches was composed in Bembo, a typeface adapted from the Monotype version of an Aldine Roman cut before 1500 by Francesco Griffo, who later designed the first italic type. It is named for Griffo's contemporary, the humanist scholar Pietro Bembo. The book was composed by Brevis Press of Bethany, Connecticut. It was designed and produced by Kachergis Book Design, Pittsboro, North Carolina.